From the
Other World

James Wright in 1972

From the Other World

Poems in Memory of James Wright

EDITED BY
Bruce Henricksen
AND **Robert Johnson**

LOST HILLS BOOKS
DULUTH, MINNESOTA

© 2008 Bruce Henricksen

All rights reserved. Unless otherwise noted on a specific page, no portion of this publication may be reproduced or transmitted in any form or by any means, electronic or mechanical, including photocopying, recording, or capturing on any information storage and retrieval system, without permission in writing from the publisher, except by a reviewer, who may quote brief passages in a critical article or review to be printed in a magazine or newspaper, or electronically transmitted on radio, television, or the Internet.

Published by:
Lost Hills Books
P.O. Box 3054
Duluth, MN 55803
www.losthillsbooks.com

First edition 2008
Cover photo: iStockPhoto
Author photo: John Unterecker
Book design: Dorie McClelland, Spring Book Design
Cover design: Cathy Spengler, Cathy Spengler Design
Interior typeset in Electra Std and Eureka Sans
12 11 10 09 08   1 2 3 4 5
Manufactured in Canada

ISBN-13: 978-0-9798535-1-7
ISBN-10: 0-9798535-1-6

for Annie

Contents

Introduction: At the Touch of His Hand   1

W.S. Merwin
James   5

Joe Wilkins
As I Step Over a Puddle at the End of Winter,
I Think of a Dead Ohio Poet   6

Richard Hugo
Last Words to James Wright   8

Sander Zulauf
Your Chair in Misquamicut   11

Connie Wanek
A Field of Barley   13

Geoffrey Brock
Father Countries   15

James P. Lenfestey
Joaquin Murieta   16

Stanley Plumly
Lapsed Meadow   17
The James Wright Annual Festival   19

Galway Kinnell
Middle Path   21
Last Holy Fragrance   23

Barbary Chaapel
   Sweet Land   28
   Isla de Pasqua   29

Christina Lovin
   Two   30

Susan North
   Blue Horses   31

Gina Tabasso
   Seeing God   33

Barton Sutter
   The Stallion   35

C.K. Williams
   On Learning of a Friend's Illness   36

David Budbill
   Also   39

Rick Hilles
   Missoula Eclipse   40

Judith Pacht
   Waterville, Maine, Near Great Pond   43

Bruce Henricksen
   Now, in Minnesota   45

Sharon Chmielarz
   The Professor   46

Brenton Lee
   James Wright—A Different View   47

Gibbons Ruark
    With Our Wives in Late October   48
    Lost Letter to James Wright, With Thanks
        for a Map of Fano   50

Meena Alexander
    House of the Red Canoe   52

Diane Kendig
    The Trees Near Fiesole   53

Joyce Sutphen
    Going Someplace   54
    After That   55

Wally Swist
    Small Miracles   56

M.J. Iuppa
    Pond   57

Ellen Seussy
    The Compost Bin   58

Thomas R. Smith
    After Thanksgiving   60

Steve Troyanovich
    drifting home . . .   61

Kate Johnson
    Dayroses   62

Susan Kelly-DeWitt
    The Messenger   64

Helen Ruggieri
    The Kind of Poetry I Want   65

Michael Dennis Browne
    The Voices   66
    Shall We Gather   68

March Harshman
    Diving for the Drowned   69

Maggie Smith
    First Spring   71

Tonya Northenor
    Along the Ohio Valley   73

Nancy Paddock
    Snow Goose River   74

Robert Bly
    Canada Goose   75
    A Note on James Wright   76

Authors and credits   79

A Brief Bibliography   83

Acknowledgments

Many people have assisted this project with their encouragement and their deep love for the poetry of James Wright. They include Janet Baker, Craig Blais, John Bradley, Christopher Buckley, Edward Byrne, Hayden Carruth, Doug Cockrell, Temple Cone, Gretchen Fletcher, Trina Gaynon, Judith Hemschemeyer, Richard Holinger, Roy Jacobstein, Stephanie Kapinos, John Lehman, Joanne Lowery, Rob Merrit, Cindy Milwe, Jamie Parsley, Kenneth Parsons, David Radavich, Richard Robbins, Susan Sailer, John Savoie, Joe Paddock, Derek Sheffield, Maxine Silverman, Merry Speece, Jeanine Stevens, Mark Thalman, and Will Wells.

At the Touch of His Hand

James Wright was born in 1927 to a working-class family in Martins Ferry, Ohio, a factory town along the Ohio River. People were poor there, the air was polluted, and life was hard during the Depression. It's a landscape that haunts Wright's poetry, particularly the early books, *The Green Wall, St. Judas,* and *The Branch Will Not Break*. But Wright did not remain in Martins Ferry; he first joined the Army and then attended Kenyon College, where he studied under John Crowe Ransom, and eventually he received a Ph.D. from the University of Washington. As a graduate student, he became a close friend of Theodore Roethke.

In *James Wright: A Profile*, Peter Stitt understands Wright's career in terms of a quest that involves the loss of a primal Eden, a journey through a veil of tears, and finally a glimpse of another paradise. Industrialized America—the environs of his childhood—is the setting for the veil of tears, whereas the beauties of nature offer intimations of another realm. Often a poem by Wright transforms what is immediate and particular into what is other worldly and paradisiacal. As he says in "Milkweed":

>   . . . At the touch of my hand,
>   The air fills with delicate creatures
>   From the other world.

The delicate creatures released by the poet's hand may be the denizens of his lost Eden—"whatever it was I lost, whatever I wept for."

James Wright won the Pulitzer Prize in 1972 for his *Collected Poems*. In the course of time, Italy became his new-found paradise, where he and his second wife, Annie, traveled so often during the years after the Pulitzer. If the opposition between Eden and the fallen world provides a useful mapping of Wright's poetry, an equally important opposition is between the aesthetic realm and the social. Wright's poetry challenges America's social values while at the same time stepping away from them into another world of untainted beauty. Sometimes beauty provides a needed solace, but not always. No poem establishes these poles more powerfully than "To a Blossoming Pear Tree," the title poem of his eighth book, and none makes a choice more clearly.

In the first stanza of this poem the pear tree embodies pure, detached beauty. The second stanza, in contrast, describes the poet's encounter with an aging and desperate man on a Minneapolis street corner in the dead of winter. Eventually, the poet realizes that the pear tree—which is to say beauty alone—cannot alleviate human suffering. The poem ends with the speaker's discovery that:

> . . . the dark
> Blood in my body drags me
> Down with my brother.

Sympathetic portraits of society's outcasts and criminals recur in Wright's work. One of the best examples is the title poem of his second book, "St. Judas." This poem, a sonnet (the traditional form of the love poem), is spoken by Judas after the Betrayal. On his way to hang himself, Judas comes upon a man beaten by a gang of thugs.

> Then I remembered bread my flesh had eaten,
> The kiss that ate my flesh. Flayed without hope,
> I held the man for nothing in my arms.

For an act of love that has escaped public notice, society's outcast becomes Wright's saint.

Elegies by Wright's peers, many of them brought together in one place in *From the Other World*, testify to his towering presence in the poetry of late twentieth-century America. Mingling with them on these pages are poems by a younger generation of poets influenced by James Wright. Readers with knowledge of Wright's poetry, or with a copy of his poems at hand, will enjoy seeing how these influences work.

For instance, the poem by Joe Wilkins is an homage to the opening poem in "The Branch Will Not Break," while poems by Connie Wanek and Geoffrey Brock give sympathetic glimpses of Cain that echo Wright's portrait of Judas. Christina Lovin's poem refers directly to Wright's "A Blessing," where two horses love one another in their utter loneliness, while Barton Sutter seems to take issue with the idyllic quality of that poem. Williams's elegy also references "The Blessing," but now the blessing has passed, not only because Wright is gone but because the industrialism that he lamented has further blighted the land.

This collection began in conversations between the two editors. Both attended the University of Minnesota during Wright's teaching days there, and both stumbled in similar fashion on *The Branch Will Not Break* in the old Co-op Bookstore on University Avenue. Robert and Bruce did not know one another in those days and were only recently introduced by Lucy Vilankulu, editor of *Minnesota Literature*. So Lucy has something to do with this book, too.

While James Wright is first and always a poet of Ohio, there is much of Minnesota in his work—the homeless in Minneapolis and St. Paul, the Walker Art Center crowd, the farms off the road to Rochester, and the rivers and lakes. He is important in the memories of the editors and of many others who sat in his classes at the University of Minnesota, at Macalister College in St. Paul, and later at Hunter College in New York, and of course in the memories of people who found his poems in other places.

He showed us our damaged world and another, longed-for world as well. He taught us to see beauty without ignoring suffering, and in doing so he helped us to live. Thank you, Jim.

W.S. Merwin

James

News comes that a friend far away
is dying now

I look up and see small flowers appearing
in spring grass outside the window
and can't remember their name

"James," copyright © 2005 W.S. Merwin, is reprinted with the permission of the Wylie Agency Inc.

Joe Wilkins

As I Step Over a Puddle at the End of Winter, I Think of a Dead Ohio Poet

James Wright, balding old poet,
What's the use?
I think of you
Young, skulking the mud banks of the Ohio,
Slinging hunks of sumac far out
To deep water, watching them drift
And snag in the raspberry brambles,
While the coal stacks of Wheeling Steel
Split the sky in two.

But it is 2005, almost spring again,
And the highways of Montana
Build me my own black river
Of sumac and raspberry.
Where is Dick Hugo, the friend you loved?
Where is the tall grass that once solved the whole loneliness
Of the West? Where is Billings? The throats
Of the beet stacks breathing smoke? I can see nothing
But a rim of stone and a far prairie
Darkening with winter.

Yet even now,
The sky swings back to itself in the puddle's
Shattered face and I remember
You made it.
Forgive me if I follow
The footpath down the gravel banks
Of the river, through the hobo jungle weeds,
On past the hinged and reeling silks of spiders,
Where the last daylight swirls with dust–
Old poet, I'll follow you
All through your ruins.

Richard Hugo

Last Words to James Wright

I'll call you Bedford, Ed. That's what you called me.
The plane lifts off the runway, circles left across
the mountains, straightens and heads east.
I'm reading in New York and Zetta's coming.
Ed was you, was me, our private ploy.
He lasted thirty years. Now one of Ed is gone.
And what's one Ed alone? You told me January 3
they'd operate in time and damn it, Jim,
I took that as a promise. I really did.
Ed Bedford, you bastard, you lied.

This time, the branch is broke. In early work
you urged the criminal, the derelict,
the dispossessed to run between the stars.
You wanted words to sing the suffering on
and every time you asked the words came willing.
I'm toasting you in heaven, four miles over Billings.
When I see Zetta, your wife,
I'll kiss her. I'll call her Annie for luck.
I'm scared as hell nothing's going to work.
Ed Bedford, you bastard, you lied.

You're the only man I knew outside of me
quoted Robert Benchley, same passages in fact.
You need every laugh you get
when your home town's stocked with broken souls.
You left and couldn't leave that dirty river town
where every day the dirty river rolls.
I'll toast you on the Minneapolis layover.
As Rodney Dangerfield puts it, Ed:
"It's not easy, life. Not easy at all."
Make it scotch and dirty river water.

Now the New York leg, non stop. The Midwest
moves back in the dark, now and then
the dull electric burn of town, the dark again.
Off left, some shining major city. Remember, Jim,
when they seemed glamorous, filled with magnificent women
you'd never find at home. That and the need to run,
the gift that sent a raw boy non stop
over a green wall, over a green world,
star to star, buddy to dubious saints.
What poet ever found a synonym for shame?

Those saints in solitary where the dirty river rolls,
they know each life clicks off and on,
the off darker than a shabby habit,
the on more blinding than a stray star in the kitchen.
Jesus, Jim, the starker the fact I'm facing
the less I want to sing. Sorry, Ed,
to be so goddamn serious. We've got your poems.
We've all got at least two names.
But which one gives and keeps his word?
Ed Bedford, you bastard, you lied.

Ed Bedford, you bastard, you died.
What a chill. We circle the Statue of Liberty.
I feel no liberty at all on the final approach.
I feel a little drunk and a lot more empty,
like passing through some unknown factory town
knowing it must be home.
Be glad of the green wall you climbed across one day.
Be glad as me.
I forgive you, Ed, even if I did swear never.
What's a lie between Eds? What's one more dirty river?

"Last Words to James Wright," from *Making Certain It Goes On: Collected Poems of Richard Hugo* by Richard Hugo. Copyright © 1984 by The Estate of Richard Hugo. Used by permission of W. W. Norton & Company, Inc.

Sander Zulauf

Your Chair in Misquamicut

In Memoriam, James Wright

Annie hands me your chair this morning
Unfolding it into bright sunlight and heavy dew
And you join us under Giotto-blue skies
Hung out to dry after last night's thunder showers.
Your spirit rebukes suffering and memory
And you're cheered by the ease of the cricket's
Sweet babbling, the chickadee's frenetic
Reedy singing of its name,
That one dark velvety violet
Poking wild through the patio's pebbles,
The fruits of one more summer
Ripening and gone,
Tomatoes, peppers, eggplants, portulacas,
Marigold, scaevola, tuberous begonia,
Petals parted and pollen
Milked by burly longshoremen
Crawling into balsam, into zucchini
Flowers, their legs
Laden with living gold,
Flying off to another, again, again, another,
That pair of cardinals
Relishing the cantaloupe seeds

Annie's thrown under the feeder for them
To share with the mockingbirds,
Your chair, the brackets
Rusted now, webbing
Shredded and hanging down
Under a new canvas cover
Fastened to the aluminum frame,
Poetry strong enough to hold us
Throughout this lifetime's
Sacrament of praise.

Connie Wanek

A Field of Barley

Wind passes over a field of barley.
Nothing could be more lyrical.
Why God favored Abel's burnt meat
I'll never understand.

Sometimes I imagine the hills of Nod
covered with barley, and Cain standing alone,
dark with sunburn, wondering
what more he must do to be forgiven.

Years ago I visited a blooming orchard
on the east slope of the mountains
watered by its own spring, and I thought
I'd surely found Eden.

At night we saw city lights glowing
far out in the plain,
but the dark rock rose behind the farm,
eternal and absolute.

Up there one could see tragedy
long before it arrived,
foreshadowed in the first act.
Dust swelled behind its four wheels.

Dread is our inheritance.
But what sprouts out of the earth
is our consolation, the good yellow grain,
heavy in our arms.

Geoffrey Brock

Father Countries

The first true human, Cain was born in sorrow.
Adam covered his ears as his son crowned;
Eve had fathomed her curse. Cain made no sound.
Cain the man cleared the chamomile and yarrow,
Conceived the scythe, the digging stick, the furrow,
Coaxed wheat and emmer from the wounded ground,
And sacrificed. Searching the sky, Cain found
Only god's vast back turned, spined by a sparrow.

The first to kill, the first to be unbrothered,
Cain ached to see God's face, even in anger.
Some sheep came wandering by; they ate the wheat.
A spotted moon rose; all the emmer withered.
Cain, soon to father countries of pure hunger,
Slaughtered a lamb and salted its bright meat.

James P. Lenfestey

Joaquin Murieta

The trail forks left through scrub
no higher than a man
toward the south fork of the creek.

A brown sign, lazy, bent, reads
"Murieta's Camp."

Has the Forest Service finally
found your outlaw traces, Joaquin?

You the Anglos never caught, never tortured,
never hanged but in their dreams?

You who rode upon them
bright-eyed in their nightmares

and took it back.

Took it back, California.
Took it back, mountains and rivers.
Took it back, gold and silver.
Took it back, slaughtered tribes
and beaten women

who loved you,
angry outlaw,
hidden in these hills.

Stanley Plumly

Lapsed Meadow

    Wild has its skills.
  The apple grew so close to the ground
it seemed the whole tree
    was thicket, crab and root—

    by fall it looked
  like brush among burdock and hawkweed;
looked as if brush had been piled,
    for burning, at the center.

    At the edges, blurred,
  like failed fence, the hawthorns, by
comparison, seemed planted.
    Everywhere else there was broom

    grass and timothy
  and wood fern and sometimes a sapling,
sometimes a run of hazel. In Ohio,
    some people call it

    a farmer's field, all fireweed
  and thistle, a waste of nature. And true,
you could lose yourself
    in the mind of the thing,

especially summer, in the full
sun or later, after rain and the smell
of rain—you could lose
yourself, waste- or head-high,

branch by leaf by branch.
There could be color, the kind that opens
and the kind that closes up,
one for each part

of the light; there might
be fruit, green or grounded—it was always
skin-tight, small and hard.
There would be goldenrod

still young or yellowing
in season, and wind enough to seed a countryside
of plows and pasture.
But I call it crazy

the way that apple,
in the middle of a field, dug in, part of the year
bare-knuckled, part of the year
blossoming.

for James Wright

Stanley Plumly

The James Wright Annual Festival

That night we flew into Pittsburgh where Tom Flynn met the plane to drive us back to Ohio just over the river into Belmont County where we were to meet Galway and the hosts of the Second Annual James Wright Festival for supper and the chatter of a late night before the first day of readings. What I remember from the long ride in from the airport—a new spring night with constellations broken and the blurred edges of the foothills building against the wind in a wall up from the river—is the dark and how it came into the car at a speed we understood, how it filled in the small lights going out everywhere behind us, how it moved on our faces; how later, after dinner, all of us tiring, it touched all our faces. What I remember from Galway's face that night is how the next day he talked about the work, up until the end, on the last book, or didn't talk but got lost in the moment of the last poem of *that Venice morning many times since*, and how he waited there, in thought, with the many sources. On the Sunday I spent the empty early morning wandering too, lost in Martins Ferry, where down the street from the library the Heslop Brothers were still in business and farther still the WPA Swimming Pool Project plaque shone like a war memorial object. And I walked down to the water, the beautiful Ohio, Depression-wide all the way to Wheeling, and saw

that whatever the working terrors are they are worse over
there, on the other side, laid off, sabbath or dead-time on
the line, where hell is still a foundry and a glassworks and
an icehouse filled with coal, where they take you, out of
pity, in the morning before daylight and bring you back
in the evening, fire in the sun, white-of-the-eye-of-the-
moon; and that even the petty farmers, our fathers, had
come down from the farms to cross. James Wright, Galway
would finally say, had gone to the end of the table, which
we will earn, as we earn the daily bread set before us, and
in Galway's face, in the room of the gathered that day, you
could see the winter daybreak poem take form, in a whole
other country, in high gold Mediterranean air but lifted
here like stone or lumber flat above the river.

Galway Kinnell

Middle Path

Let James rejoice with the Skuttle-Fish,
  who foils his foe by the effusions of his ink.
                                        Christopher Smart

One at a time your feet lift,
and slide through the air, and stamp
down with the awkward gait
of someone who has been wound up
too tight somewhere and set down
and pointed in the directions
of inner and outer, both together—

past fallen trees that hold up their root-
systems for psychiatric inspection,
past singers who flash the pink of their tonsils,
dogs who hoist a leg but drizzle on themselves,
beggarmen eager to tell their life stories,
Boeing wings that lower their landing flaps
and reveal the tiny whirling gears,
cash registers that cry *Treblinka!*
when the cash drawer pops open—everything
found a way to show you its insides
in those days when you walked on Middle Path on fire

in the clear idea that it could be done—
but, since speech that expresses trouble
takes going through hell, also afraid
that it could not be done for long.

You of all of us were to be able to sit
down forever, almost without self,
with pencil and notebook, with second sight,
wherever life and death meet.

Today, this first day of spring,
I can see you stray off Middle Path,
lifting your feet high to stomp through
the last sooted remains of snow, and move
among the ancient graves, and hunker down
at the headstone, and read the chisellings time
and the chemical rains have spared:

> *Alfred and* [effaced]
>   *Age 6   Age 4*
> *Children of* [effaced] *and Elizabeth* [effaced]
> *Of such is the kingdom of* [effaced]

Galway Kinnell

Last Holy Fragrance

In memoriam James Wright

When by first light I went out
from the last house on the chemin de Riou
to start up the cistern pump, I saw him,
mumbling into his notebook
while the valley awakened: a cock
called full force, a car's gears
mis-shifted, a dog made feeble yaps.
The next winter in Mt. Sinai,
tufted with the stubble that sticks out
of chins on skid row in St. Paul,
Minnesota, he handed me the poem
of that Venice morning. Many times since
I have said it and each time heard
his voice saying it under mine,
and in fact in those auditoriums
that don't let you hear yourself, sometimes
I hear *only* his voice, surprising language
a little with the mourning
that goes on inside it for what it names,
and surprising himself too, making
his eyes pop a little, showing the whites.

This is also the monotony of poetry,
the droning rhythmic mutter of it,
as oblivious to emotion as the printed page,
that is older than any poem, that the song men
of Arnhem Land, who jolt their clapsticks
with a rebuking force, like a spank,
summon, or the shaman in Point Barrow,
Alaska, having trance-learned it, translates,
or gopher frogs put to us in *parallelismus membrorum*,
or, now and then, a poem resonates with:
those last, tragic, farewell poems of his,
that overtake the chant and synchronize
with its joy, in mourning's morning.

"How am I ever going to be able to say this?
The truth is there is something terrible,
almost unspeakably terrible in our lives,
and it demands respect, and, for some reason
that seems to me quite insane, it doesn't hate us.
There, you see? Every time I try
to write it down it comes out gibberish."

He lies back fast asleep in the airplane seat.
Under his eyelids consciousness flickers.
A computation: the difference, figured
in a flash, between what has already been lived
and what remains to be. He dreams it could be
of whittling a root, transfiguring it
by subtraction—of whatever it is in roots
that makes them cling—perhaps into a smile,
like that one now passing his lips, or into

a curled up, oriental death's body
mummified into the memories of last visitors.
Even asleep his face sweats. SS
Torturers start working Cagney over. He knows
he will crack and spill the invasion plans.
But he hears the rumbling of bombers
come to shut his mouth, and cracks a grin.
When the bombs explode he madly laughs.
Sitting up, he peers out the plane window
to see if we might be coming in too low,
as if preparing to laugh among the screams.

For this poet, the blessed moment
was not only at last, in Fano, in spring,
where, with his beloved Annie, just before
returning home to die, he got well,
but also at first, forty years earlier,
by the Ohio, where he sat and watched
the river flow, and flowed himself inside it,
humming and lulling first beginnings
that would heal not only his own self
but all the solitares who sprawl on sidewalks
like dropped flowers waiting to be lady-slippered
into first perfume or last stink, or squat
in their own leakage on curbstones,
watching paper trash gyre spellbound a block
or so and fall back, trash again, or stand on a windy
corner, gesticulating and talking to nobody.

The computation darkens. Again
and again it used to show plenty of time.
Now, even on the abacus of the rosary,
or the petals, hushed to the table top, of roses,
which we mortal augurers figure and refigure
out on our incredulous infinity of times,
it comes out: a negative number. Fear,
the potion of death, is yet a love derivative,
and some terrible pinch of it must be
added to restore the power to cling.

Near where it first forms,
the Ohio stops in its bed and baptizes under ice
all its creatures, even the boy sitting soon
in nobody's memory some days downriver.
He went away, three-quarters
whittled root of silenus wood,
taking a path that, had it vanished,
we could imagine kept going, toward a place
where he waits to rise again into
the religion of the idolatry of images
graven their moment into being-born-and-dying.

The path ends there where the white rose
lies on top of its shadow in Martins Ferry,
Ohio, let drop on her way by a child too stunned
by dead bells pounding through sunlight
to hold it, or anything, or anyone, tight
that day, giving up its last holy fragrance
into this ending-time, when the earth
lets itself be shoveled open to take in a body.

It will be a long time before anyone is born
who can lull as he could the words
he will now not ever use—words which,
now he has left, turn this way and that—
hum and coax them to press up against, shape
themselves by, know, true-love, and idolize.

"The Middle Path" and "Last Holy Fragrance," from *Strong Is Your Hold*: Poems by
Galway Kinnell. Copyright © 2006 by Galway Kinnell. Reprinted by permission of
Houghton Mifflin Company. All rights reserved.

Barbary Chaapel

Sweet Land

Landscape shaped his life and death.
Silken mist at day's beginning,
Black-bottomed clouds at four o'clock.
Summery heat in between.
Roy Smith rose to cornbread
Made with water. A cup of chicory coffee.
He walked with hoe to the cornfield
To hill one thousand ankle-high stalks
Of green against green.
He worked until eleven,
Dropped his hoe to get a drink,
Water at the springhouse
Beneath the beechnut tree . . .
And made it as far as the clothesline
Where he struggled to stand upright
While his heart excavated itself.
Winters past he'd scrabbled coal
On his knees from an earthen hole.
It must have been like that just then,
His heart filling with frozen, hot coals
As he called my grandma's name.

Barbary Chaapel

Isla de Pasqua

The choir of women
Turned to stone
For they believed

In the power of silence,
In the powerful silence
Of their own stillness.

Sculpted heads,
Eyes carved with obsidian hand tools,
Swallowed-tongue women
On that island called Easter.

Cipher the message:
Wind in the trees, raindrops
Speak for me, their sister:
I am stillness.

Before the sharp tongue of my love
My power, too, lies
In words unspoken.

So impassioned,
Sometimes
He calls me stone.

Christina Lovin

Two

They love each other.
There is no loneliness like theirs.
    James Wright, "A Blessing"

Now there are two. Seven deer, I'm told, before
the cougar's appetite growled: one by one they were taken
down to the forest's soft floor. Just these two escaping:
a tale told by the ragged ear of the one, the nervous
watching by the other. But now they still themselves.
Aware that I am near they do not startle, barely move
across the grass, pause like warm brown statues framed
against trees nearly black in the dusk, but silvery
with mist near their tops. I cough, reminded of my own
frail life, but still the deer do not scare beyond a stare
in my direction. There are two: just enough to take care
of the business of grooming. They stand neck-to-neck,
each licking, nuzzling, teasing the ticks and lice from the other's
coarse fur, enjoying the comfort, the contact, as horses do.
As do humans. As do you; as do I. Touch me here, then,
softly as deer's breath. I will touch you there, where
your mother held you in her arms, your neck against her shoulder.
Not where the raging fire begins, where undergrowth sparks
and catches and we are lost in its blaze. No, here,
where the hushed forest opens and the two quiet bodies
have disappeared into the green darkness within.

Susan North

Blue Horses

Already it's not going
by the book. The mare's
in trouble and I remember
more of your hands than today.
She's been waxed up since Monday,
the foal diving in her belly
like a hooked fish. I wish
I were just animal. I'd let you
slowly undress me and not worry
for order in the universe.
She's wearing a circle
in the field, pawing, sweating.
The great white and brown body
is a mountain. Labor
takes her down in its fist.
If she were less strong,
she could die more easily.
I won't think about your wife
or how long before you come again.
I would never color inside the lines
or use the green the nuns named grass.
My sky was yellowpurple, unrepentant
as a bruise. Blue horses kept me
after school. Even now it is the same.

We take the consequence of what we see,
owe the colors everything. By evening
the mare will be buried or nursing.
If you drive in, I will be feeding chickens
or stretching fence in the last light.
When we go to the kitchen, I will turn
to the sink, cold well water running
clear and hard across both arms.
You will come up behind me,
placing your right hand
on the counter, your left on my hip.
Whatever I pay for this is too little.

Gina Tabasso

Seeing God

I will never stop telling you I love you
because you have seen me ride my horse
and called us "God,"
seen cancer move through your mother's blood
and been brave enough to love other women,
seen a bullet lodged in the flesh
of your left hip and continued walking,
seen the way I deal with death and held it
in your arms so I could kiss the soul
as it left the body. You have looked into
my eyes full of tears and shown me those in your own.

I will never stop telling you how beautiful
I find the way you wear boots with the steel
showing through the toe; your knees flashing
cratered moons through jeans when you rock
back on your heels; hands wrapped around
wrapping paper rolls, shot glasses, power tools,
breasts; spread open on the bed as if Delilah
never betrayed Sampson or Judith didn't walk away
with Holofernes's head, I will kiss both
your cheeks with no thought of betrayal.

I will never stop telling you your breath tastes sweet
in the morning, your sweat makes you more real,
your scent on my blankets the only lullaby
I need during the nights you're afraid to sleep
like a man who only has days to live.

I will not stop telling you to love yourself
like gladiolas do when they open, like morning glories
as they climb. Love yourself as simply as soap
and water, as easily as loving me comes,
as honestly as seeing god in a horse.

I will always love only you
Because I have sat on my horse and felt
the god run through him, electricity
rumble under the skin. I have sat
with my knees on each side your smooth hip
and the scarred one, felt the same quiver
run from the top of your head, down past your heart,
up into mine.

Barton Sutter

The Stallion

Walking the dry winter woods,
I reached the hidden pasture
And paused to admire the mare and stud
Till he came after me, the bastard.

He ran right at me, reared,
And whipped around to kick.
I hollered, "Hyah!" but he didn't hear,
So I retreated, throwing sticks.

He'd always been shy and mild,
But the mare was so fat with his foal
He'd suddenly grown wild,
Proud as a prince, powerful.

He chased me half a mile
Till I rolled beneath a fence.
He stood there sweating, male,
Magnificent. I dusted off my pants.

"So long," I said, "you son of a bitch."
And headed home. The sky was red and violet.
Reeds and cattails rattled in the ditch.
I felt a wonderful violence.

C.K. Williams

On Learning of a Friend's Illness

for James Wright

The morning is so gray that the grass is gray and the side of the white horse grazing
is as gray and hard as the harsh, insistent wind gnawing the iron surface of the river,
while far off on the other shore, the eruptions from the city seem for once more docile and benign
than the cover of nearly indistinguishable clouds they unfurl to insinuate themselves among.

It's a long while since the issues of mortality have taken me this way. Shivering,
I tramp the thin, bitten track to the first rise, the first descent, and, toiling up again,
I startle out of their brushy hollow the whole herd of wild-eyed, shaggy, unkempt mares,
their necks, rumps, withers, even faces begrimed with patches of the gluey, alluvial mud.

All of them at once, their nostrils flared, their tails flung up over their backs like flags,
are suddenly in flight, plunging and shoving along the narrow furrow of the flood ditch,

bursting from its mouth, charging headlong towards the wires at the pasture's end,
banking finally like one great, graceful wing to scatter down the hillside out of sight.

Only the oldest of them all stays with me, and she, sway-backed, over at the knees,
blind, most likely deaf, still, when I approach her, swings her meager backside to me,
her ears flattening, the imperturbable opals of her eyes gazing resolutely over the bare,
scruffy fields, the scattered pines and stands of third-growth oak I called a forest once.

I slip up on her, hook her narrow neck, and haul her to me, hold her for a moment, let her go.
I hardly can remember anymore what there ever was out here that keeps me coming back
to watch the land be amputated by freeways and developments, and the mares, in their sanctuary,
thinning out, reverting, becoming less and less approachable, more and more the symbols of themselves.

How cold it is. The hoofprints in the hardened muck are frozen lakes, their rims atilt,
their glazed opacities skewered with straw, muddled with the ancient, ubiquitous manure.
I pick a morsel of it up: scentless, harmless, cool, as desiccated as an empty hive,
it crumbles in my hand, its weightless, wingless filaments taken from me by the wind and strewn

in a long, surprising arc that wavers once then seems to burst
   into a rain of dust.
No comfort here, nothing to say, to try to say, nothing for
   anyone. I start the long trek back,
the horses nowhere to be seen, the old one plodding wearily
   away to join them,
the river, bitter to look at, and the passionless earth, and the
   grasses rushing ceaselessly in place.

"On Learning of a Friend's Illness" from *Collected Poems* by C.K. Williams. Copyright © 2006 by C.K. Williams. Reprinted with permission of Farrar, Straus and Giroux, LLC.

David Budbill

Also

Also an Ohio boy, also working class, also
uneducated family, knowing the bitterness
of being trapped in mill town, factory town,
Martins Ferry, Cleveland, what's the diff?

Knowing also the arrogance of the elite,
the literati. Knowing how people use art
to separate themselves from ordinary
working stiffs—those out of whom we both
had come—the way we both also had done.

Also knowing more than anybody ought to
about anguish, pain, frustration of seeing
life drain into a bottle, pack of cigarettes,
assembly line, anonymity.

Thank You, James, for that day in 1963 when
I found *The Branch Will Not Break*, heard you
say, "Come back. Return. All of life and poetry
is in those people's lives that you have spent
your life running from. Come back. Return.
Dirty, gritty, dumb—and beautiful—Ohio
is where you're from."

Rick Hilles

Missoula Eclipse

> *Believe the couple who have finished their*
> *picnic/and make wet love in the grass . . .*
> *Believe in milestones, the day/you left home*
> *forever and the cold open way/a world*
> *would not let you come in.*
>
> *(Part of the inscription on Richard Hugo's headstone*
> *in Missoula, MT, from his poem, "Glen Uig.")*

If I could live again as just one thing
it would be this early Autumn wind
as it cartwheels the rooftops & avenues
of the Pacific Northwest; the way the air
of orchards vaulted in the mind of Keats
as he brimmed over with his last Odes
dreaming of the mouths his final words
would touch & kiss through any darkness

like a shooting star; the way a starry-eyed
stranger once blew smoke into the night
before offering me her cigarette outside
the 92nd Street Y, where I'd just given
a reading, so that I didn't even notice
sad-faced Jim Wright in a patch of leaves.
And there we were again, Jim weeping
& breathless to tell me he'd stopped drinking

and was in love; and, in a voice reserved
for children (and the very lost) told me
he had cancer. I wish we had hightailed it
then into my dream of Rome, the dream
where we are laughing at our dumb luck
and near giddy as we exit the gilded portal
& enter a day too bright to see the Spanish steps,
where, for us, apparently, it is always noon;

I always wanted to take Jim to Rome —
to see the black ink of cuttlefish
and shadows blue the edges of his grin
even if we were just to stand penniless & eye
the sparkling wishes tossed into fountains,
one whose water surrounds a sculpted hull
of a boat that's lost its mast, held in a state
of perpetual sinking as Jim points to the flat

where John Keats died, his friend Severn
at his side, drawing him over and over —
even after his last torment; Jim tells me
about the dream he's having lately
in which Keats appears, practically
flying up and down the Spanish Steps
in inline blades; Jim wants so badly
to grab the frilly garment of the white-

shirted Romantic, who now is naked
to the waist and in black spandex,
in death forever beautiful and ridiculous,
but Jim's afraid to wake us from the dream.
Still, there's a melody under Keats' breath.

It might be from Haydn's "Water Music"
or just the syncopated rhythms of the boat
we ride, Our Fountain of the Sinking Ship.

Oh, to be so close to the poet we love
who died at half our age not knowing
what he would become for so many of us,
understandably, makes us a little insane.
Jim asks if I know what it all means
& then he's coming at me like Sonny Liston,
as if the only way affection can be shown
between men like us is with an open fist.

And, forgetting a moment that I am
not even the merest breeze in your living hair,
and that a boneyard in Missoula, Montana
negates this vision, just now to my dead friend
I'm real as any man who's loved his life,
&, stunned by it, tries to face what he can't take,
when the trees of Rome rattle their silver leaves,
and Jim picks me up, like nothing, in his arms.

Judith Pacht

Waterville, Maine, Near Great Pond

There were woods, there were winters, summers and a girl
Lying under the elm. She was ten, a new watch on her wrist,
This was enough, this was everything.
She lay on peat from fallen leaves, her cushion of ten times ten.

She was lying under the elm, a new watch on her wrist,
The scent of resin and damp earth, musk and bark in the air,
Her cushion of ten times ten from fallen leaves
Thick and brown after years of slow-melting snow.

The scent of resin and damp earth, musk and bark hung in the air.
That day sun licked the elm leaves, licked her eyelids
As she lay on powdered leaves, thick from slow-melting snow.
A gentle wind stirred the air soft over shallows on Great Pond.

That day sun licked the elm leaves, licked her eyelids—
Though something she couldn't reach flickered by.
Wind stirred the air soft over shallows on Great Pond
Where she always swam—right over there.

Something she couldn't reach flickered by
And she thought of the sun pressing early spring to summer,
Warming where she swam, right over there
Where the lazy traffic of birds, a breeze, shook the elm.

As though the sun is pressing early spring to summer, she thought.
This is enough: the breeze, the elm, the lazy traffic of birds.
There were woods, there were winters, summers in those days.
She set her new watch to keep that time. She was ten that day.

Bruce Henricksen

Now, in Minnesota

At the edge of things time turns.
Its sound is tires on the interstate
And the squawk of gulls that wheel
Beside the lake.

Here, in the garden, it is still.
Small leaves of poplar shimmer
Like coins.

Again, the hours in their leaving touch
One's face so softly you'd almost
Think they cared.

In the shade of the oak by the fence
That old brown dog, my life,
Makes a circle of itself
And rests.

Sharon Chmielarz

The Professor

for James Wright

Three times a week he passed by
my chair, in dusty Folwell Hall.
Three times his small planet
revolved around the great sun,
Shakespeare, in that room,
pulling toward the light, picking
up underdogs in his orbit, the
fairies, Falstaffs, fat girls, drunks,
kings of lost kingdoms, three times
a week we tagged along in that
gravity, that fragile path he paced
through words and their long comets
I couldn't get enough of, though
he gave and gave and gave;
mistaken as ice, his hot surface.
I didn't know his poetry then,
the inclination planets have
toward the sun, how their paths
throw sun's light on all.
Thus seeds grow. Thus we see
how our shadows lengthen.

Brenton Lee

James Wright — A Different View

He was a great Poet
I didn't know
A Genius, some say
I never knew
He taught me things
some funny, some weird
We would visit a park
Or museum
Many years later
I learn of his greatness
Did I miss anything
No Uncle James
Not a thing

Gibbons Ruark

With Our Wives in Late October

for James Wright

Wandering with weather down the long hillside,
We come to the slender reeds in the water,
All of us who lazed by our own rivers
    Summer and autumn,

Looking for redwings or leaves that were falling,
Light that was flying, the red wing of summer,
Never dreaming to be by one sure river
    Gathered together.

Now by the slender reeds in the water
Annie and Kay are looking for spiders,
Their own thoughts slender as the thoughts of spiders
    Looking for women.

Diligent spiders are our kindred creatures,
Friends of the season, and they are raveling
Somewhere lonelier than I can follow
    With all my singing,

But here's one Annie has suddenly sighted
Loitering brightly over the water,
Letting his legged and delicate star-body
    Flash us a signal

Clearer than water or the redwing's shoulder:
Some stars in heaven already dying
Light up the moonless night that is coming,
 Some stars are other

Bodies altogether, reluctant to say
How they become the light of October,
This spider, these leaves, these loveliest
 Faces of women.

Gibbons Ruark

Lost Letter to James Wright, With Thanks for a Map of Fano

Breathing his last music, Mozart is supposed
To have said something heartbreaking which escapes me
For the quick moment of your bending to a dime

Blinking up from York Avenue, the last chill evening
I ever saw you, laughter rising with the steam
From your scarred throat, long-remembering laughter,

"Well, the old *eye* is still some good, anyway."
I thought of your silent master Samuel Johnson
Folding the fingers of drowsing vagrant children

Secret as wings over the coppers he left in their palms
Against the London cold and tomorrow's hunger.
You could not eat, I think you could scarcely swallow,

And yet that afternoon of your sleep and waking
To speak with us, you read me a fugitive passage
From a book beside your chair, something I lose all track of

Now, in this dim hour, about the late driftwood letters
Of writers and how little they finally matter.
You wrote to me last from Sirmione (of all things,

Sirmione had turned gray that morning), and it mattered.
We were together when the gray December dusk
Came down on snapshots of the view from Sirmione,

Sunlight ghosting your beard on the beach at Fano.
I had thought to write you a letter from Fano,
A letter which could have taken years to reach you

On the slow river ways of the Italian mails,
And now I write before we even come to leave.
We are going to Fano, where we may unfold this map

At a strange street corner under a window box
Of thyme gone to flower, and catch our breath remembering
Mozart breathing his last music, managing

Somehow to say in time, "And now I must go,
When I have only just learned to live quietly."
Last time I saw you, walking a little westward

From tugboats in the harbor, your voice was already breaking,
You were speaking quietly but the one plume of your breath
Was clouding and drifting west and away from Fano

Toward the river ferry taking sounding after sounding.

Meena Alexander

House of the Red Canoe

Finally an address—2205 San Marco
And a door inches from a canal where gondolas

Strut through green waters and opera singers put out to seed
Stand and moan O sole mio and other such things

And a woman with white hair, flesh shielded by a sari
Sways beside a singer in his bulging shirt.

I stand on the sidewalk next to a red canoe,
It's propped against the dry wall, upended by fate.

The world has drifts and gristle sticking to stones
And rusty rivets stuck into underwater trees.

Njangal ivida! She cries in Malayalam,
My mother tongue, ancient language of the Dravidian coast.

Back against the wall I watch the ghost trees of Venice
Pick up their roots and approach me.

Diane Kendig

The Trees Near Fiesole

I would rather leave them alone, even
In my imagination, or better still,
Leave them to you.

                        James Wright

When you left, we found a way,
those tree seeds in Italy
and me hanging out like a leaf in Ohio
where a New York poet read in Columbus
last week and sneered that you
always wrote from above it all.

I got the hell out, north,
Canada, as far foreign as I could get quick
with all my own grief. On a cliff, over
the St. Lawrence, I picked up your last journey
at six a.m., before light.
There is less and less of that.

We die of cold and not of darkness,
Unamuno said,
and still reading by eight p.m.'s
midnight oil, I can't see at first
what the dog brings me out of the dark.
A pinecone she wants me to throw. I will
after I strip the seeds and plant them
on the wind. But first, I imagine them buckeyes.

Joyce Sutphen

Going Someplace

Someday, I will be the one going to
Perugia or Peru, and then I

will understand about the Etruscan
wall in the book that is open on my

table. Someday, instead of looking out
over a meadow in late autumn where

the leaves have gone gold and the branches are
sharp as foxes on a hillside, I'll be

in Rome or Romania and will know
which coffee shop the writers write in, and

when that tall man leans over my table
I'll be in London or Londonderry,

certain that wide waters are without sound,
that pebbles make the ocean smooth. Someday

I will be lost when least I expect it,
the last passenger let onto the train,

the one who had to run alongside and
jump from the platform on to the end of

the last car; that is how close I will be
to missing it all, that's how easily

I could have been left behind forever.

Joyce Sutphen

After That

I began with the last line of one poem,
which reminded him of the beginning

of another. And so these two poems—
one about lying in a hammock at a farm

in Minnesota, the other about
a legendary head we can never

know, will always come together in my
mind. When is it too late to revise your

life? How many lives does it take to fill
a hammock? And after you have seen the

butterfly sleeping on the trunk and the
chicken hawk floating over, it must be

that your life is perfectly tuned, ready
for whatever it is comes after that.

Wally Swist

Small Miracles

Barn swallows, those dark handkerchiefs,
that drop from the sky and lift

again, find a place to perch,
then pause on a rim of a perfect arc.

I also fly into the eternity of an image
like the cricket,

that black jewel,
who sings about nothing but this all night.

M. J. Iuppa

Pond

In day's broad light, in heat, without threat of more rain,
my husband works alone, clearing
weeds and rocks near the split-rail fence.

He digs a neatly carved pit and calls it Pond,
filling its kidney shape with water and cattails,
and goldfish won at the firemen's fair.

Under the wide shade of a white umbrella,
he snakes a garden hose up under a terrace of rocks,
turning the water's spray to perpetual music.

I like to look into this pond with my weariness.
I like to watch the clouds in its quiet face.
I like to see the flash of bright orange, streaking

out of the shadows
to somewhere just beyond my sight.

Ellen Seusy

The Compost Bin

All winter, and in all seasons,
I feed this dirt from my own kitchen,
taking the long walk into a deep yard.

Out of the yellow light of the house,
stepping down from the din of appliances,
out of rooms stuffy with television,

I sink into a pool of light on the snow
and pause to balance two bowls
heavy with limp celery and red cabbage.

At the edge of the light, I look down,
then step into Ohio's dark night,
into what used to be forest.

The yard is quiet. This cold walk through the dark
takes me far. Who knows what will bloom
from what I bring? At the wooden bin

I tip the bowls onto the snow-covered compost.
Chemistry is going on in there
that I don't understand; pink peonies

could come from this decay. Sometimes
I wish not to go back, but to stay out
by the soft-armed hemlocks,

out here by the compost bin,
this hearth way in the back of the yard,
and deep inside, the fire that no one lit.

Thomas R. Smith

After Thanksgiving

1.
I drive through small farming towns strung
along the road like beads. Coming down a long
hill, I see houses in the blue dusk.
The glow of the first gas station cheers me.

2.
On the main street only a bar is open,
everyone else home, having supper. . . .
Holiday lights in the greenhouse
windows gather warmth in solitude.

3.
West of town now, the sun almost gone.
Fields sink down with their lone, bare trees.
An old melancholy draws me on like
a cow to its barn across a darkening pasture.

Steve Troyanovich

drifting home . . .

It's silence I hear and obey
That I may lose my way
And myself.
       Edward Thomas

there is no other loneliness
like the eyes of twilight
finding memory
in soft shadow tangled
between stillness and
the muted passing
of autumn fields . . .

does the snow scream
clawed by empty wings?
cold starlight undresses
a december moon
while on the road between
martins ferry and new athens
i find no angels —
nightway's odometer
measuring only the distance
from lonelier to lost . . .

Kate Johnson

Dayroses

As for the pewter pitcher, it was filled
and poured out. Each life, clear
and deep as this water, and gone
before we could drink to the quench.

> As for sorrow, let it be wild plumes
> from the walking birds, the striding
> flamingo, the ostrich's tail;
> as for sorrow, find it in the white tufts
> that grow on the antelope's soft belly—
> let its delicacy sear us

until we can't forget to write
the letter L every morning
with an index finger, on the air, write
the letters D and S and B
for each daughter, sister, brother. Don't we burn
from the sheer mystery
that we are here at all?—and carry
inside us the blackened candles
of those we've loved. Water
from the silver brim poured
into our dripping hands . . . We know

they can't come back, but "knowing"
is nothing: pollen scattered
while the heart continues to grip
the flower itself; terror may try
but it can't unfist that bloom—so,
they have left us, here
with rife colors bending
in the fields and, from the pitcher,
water's emptying prayer:

> Lord, be a lace that binds us to the dead
> tighter and tighter as evening comes
> and the dayroses fold,
> and our lips close
> and only our hearts gape open
> blindly

expecting to see that familiar outline, any moment,
coming up the walk, the white gate wide—
torture us, God, while we are the living,
torture us with hope.

Susan Kelly-DeWitt

The Messenger

Last night
the messenger appeared
and I greeted him
coldly.

Which way? he asked.

After that I sank deeper
into my ruinous drowse

while the crickets chattered
in the willows by the river
and the fireflies conversed
in a teahouse lit

by their own golden lamps.
When I woke, I had forgotten
the directions I gave—

whether he turned
to follow them,
or stayed.

The crickets had quieted;
the fireflies had flown home.

I woke beside you, confused
and alone.

Helen Ruggieri

The Kind of Poetry I Want

from a line by James Wright

I want poetry from a grown woman
who's forgiven her children for getting old

I want poetry pure as a peeled bud of garlic
hot on the tongue—strong on the breath

I want poetry from a woman who smiles with her teeth
you know her—she thinks like a man

I want poetry damp and shady:
trillium, bracken and fern

The kind of poetry I want takes my shape
not even knowing my name

It is a debt forgiven
payment in kind, unkind, lonely, true

The poetry I want is high priced
and tightly wound, mean and free,

hawk high, duck deep.
I want it all in my feathery palms.

Michael Dennis Browne

The Voices

*for Dale Warland and the singers
on the occasion of their farewell concert,*
May 30, 2004

I don't know if we have ever deserved
   the voices, but they are ours,
I don't know if we ever have known
   what it means to be able to speak
in those tongues, and only
   in my worst, most useless moments
have I tried to imagine
   our lives without them.
Where might we go in the world
   where they would not reach us?

I would never go into the dark
   without the voices,
I have come to rely on how they mend us
   among the ruins
of what we have hoped for.
   If there were only one branch in the world,
the voices would find it.

Doubt was never the root of us,
    doubt winds itself, again and again,
around our doing,
    but it was never the source,
joy is the source,
    foliage of joy in which
the singers are hidden, but heard;
    always the gate, always the garden,
always the light, the shadows,
    always the leaves.

From where I stand now,
    I cannot see every singer,
but looking out across the years,
    listening in ways learned
only from them,
    I can hear all the song.

Michael Dennis Browne

Shall We Gather

where twisted lengths of girders
  lie along the river bank
they seem like scraps of sky
  that dropped, dragging
its birds with them

and these were people
  unknown, loved,
who flew awhile
  (as everyone dreams to do)
in this world of falling

Marc Harshman

Diving For the Drowned

for James Wright: In Memoriam

Off the river and up the hill into Ferry,
my first time beyond the four-lane to downtown:
brick and glass, The 5 Roses, Dutch Henry's
Novelties, the turreted bank,
the strung stop light centering town, and
overhead the airplane trailing its letters—
Bob Sumner // County Clerk—
a good day to advertise, a dark, shingled sky
only here and there licked white
with racing clouds, a good background
for words, the letters only occasionally tipping out of sight,
a good background, the valley direct and unmistakably American,
the crowded squeeze of houses between hill and river,
between factories and rocks, coal and smoke,
the kind of place you want to leave but never do.
Small towns like this hold on forever,
their close blanket of sweat, their tight rooms of mold
and cold where you try to sleep, their everybody-knows-you
faces flashing everywhere you turn on the brick-rumpled streets,
but there were heroes, ones who knew something,
who knew the under-river and found the lost,
the river's stink a pale skin of rot upon them,

the ones who came back living, rising
with stories from that dive
into the greensilver and silent current,
who had reached into that liquid night and rose
having touched death with life
yet having brought no answer
but the persistent one that lives with the telling,
the return of words
that keep us
close to each other,
the ones you fought for, the ones you made us believe
worth fighting for.

Maggie Smith

First Spring

Delaware, Ohio

The Olentangy is the closest I come
to knowing a river. Its choppy water
bubbles like spit, breaks

around birch limbs, the rounded
ruins of a limestone wall.
Passing through the scent

of chives and lilacs, I see nothing
but leaves and dappled cows
nosing the slender grasses.

I imagine stealing corn
from the fields, pulling the pale
blond strands from its pearly buttons.

As a child, I broke buckeyes
open with rocks and peeled back
the shells, rich and brown

as polished wood. I imagined
their poison meat would taste
as I thought marrow

would taste, mealy, and bitter
as human bone. Now this place,
with its spare, violent beauty,

breaks me open. I resign to spring
and its trappings: dark, bloodied
scraps of fur in the shoulders

of Bean Oller Road. Stones
begging to be turned. Everywhere,
the scent of lilacs and no sign of them.

Tonya Northenor

Along the Ohio Valley

These are the streams flooding our blood:
green hills sway into storm-clouds above a tainted river,
country lanes wind around old farm-lines.
We are sawdust and turn-and-run mares,
factory smokestacks obscuring a gold petal of sun.
Follow me along snail paths and sagging fence posts
to the glass-and-pulp heart of the city's
loud bass, rattling soda-cans, and sunset neon.
Through to the other side, where dryer sheets gather the call
of hounds on long, rusting chains.

Let us tell our story: it is lengthy as the Milky Way
we can still see when the lights are not too bright.
It is brief as the wake of a goose, a few notes fast fading.
We stand on blue front-porches, shielding our eyes,
but aching to pull it all further inside.

Nancy Paddock

Snow Goose River

all night they pass
under the sinking moon
following the bright Missouri
from Sand Lake and the snow

joy-cries in the cold
and coyotes answer
beneath Orion's wheel   hunting
until dawn

with light
honeying their wings
snow geese are waves
of the pale sky

they circle
a slow spiraling galaxy
sucked down into the same slough
thousands and thousands
of geese and years

a current
deep as their blood
drawn by summer across the world
their bodies   in flight
outline the shifting mountains
of the air

Robert Bly

The Canada Goose

What if the Canada goose calling
Disconsolately all night
Was—not Jim Wright—but
The lostness of Jim Wright,

Or yours, calling across
The rising sunshine on
The other side of the river,
Where all the stories

We told became trout;
And all the poems
We left in the river
Became the lost

Comedies of the Romans.

Robert Bly

A Note on James Wright

I first met James Wright in 1958 or 9, after I sent him a copy of the first issue of *The Fifties*. On its inside front cover I had the printer set: "All the poetry written today in the United States is too old-fashioned." James Wright was not offended by this impudence, but wrote a long, anguished letter, and shortly after visited the farm where I was living. We were both in misery over our work.

I found him a person of great artistic scrupulosity. I mean that he wanted every experience he had to be transformed before it got out onto the page. The unscrupulous put an experience into a poem the same day without altering it. An old prophet said that if you give a man some money when you go away, and ask him to save it for you, and he buries it in the ground, so saving it, he is unscrupulous. The man who risks it and makes more is not. Amazing! I suppose it is unscrupulous to simply retell an experience because all the snail and grasshoppers and hummingbirds that come to us have gone through enormous transformations to get here. So what are we to do? Visit our grandfather one day, and write a poem the next?

I was with him one time walking about the farm chatting, hovering around an old granary. I absent-mindedly opened a three foot by three foot wooden door about five feet off the ground and hooked shut. A few years ago it had been boarded over on the inside, to keep oats from pushing out through the door, and so there was an enclosed space in it. As it turned out a squirrel had decided to set up quarters there. When I pulled back the door, we saw, puzzled, a squirrel's tail poking out from the mass of corn-shucks. An instant later the cornhusks exploded and with an amazing Olympic leap the squirrel came out straight up, caught the siding, climbed straight up the granary wall, up the roof and leapt to a tree.

Jim gave no hint at all, as we looked at each other astounded, laughing, that he was going to write a poem. This is how it came out.

> As the plump squirrel scampers
> Across the roof of the corncrib,
> The moon suddenly stands up in the darkness,
> And I see that it is impossible to die.
> Each moment of time is a mountain.
> An eagle rejoices in the oak tree of heaven,
> Crying
> *This is what I wanted.*

I don't know how he does that. His power of transformation is so strong I look at his lines amazed. I see where a line came from—as in the Hammock poem—and then I see other worlds it suggests when he has worked with it. He has a brief prose poem about some lions, probably seen in a movie, lolling about on the Serengeti Plain. He writes calmly of the male, and the energy of the female lion, the color, the lazy ease. He doesn't end, "What nice lions." He says, "Small wonder Jesus wept at a human city."

Authors and credits

page 5: "James," copyright © 2005 W.S. Merwin, is reprinted with the permission of the Wylie Agency Inc.

page 6: Joe Wilkins has published poems in numerous literary magazines. He teaches at Waldorf College in Forest City, Iowa. "As I Step Over . . ." appears here for the first time.

page 8: "Last Words to James Wright," from *Making Certain It Goes On: Collected Poems of Richard Hugo* by Richard Hugo. Copyright © 1984 by The Estate of Richard Hugo. Used by permission of W. W. Norton & Company, Inc.

page 11: "Your Chair in Misquamicut" was published in *To Life: Occasions of Praise*, an anthology from Ruth Moon Kempher's Kings Estate Press, 2002. Sander Zulauf teaches at County College of Morris in New Jersey.

page 13: "A Field of Barley" is from *Hartley Field* by Connie Wanek. Reprinted with the permission of Holy Cow! Press.

page 15: "Father Countries" is from Geoffrey Brock's *Weighing Light: Poems* (Ivan Dee Row, 2005). Geoffrey teaches at the University of Arkansas in Fayetteville.

page 16: James P. Lenfestey has published several books of poems. "Joaquin Murieta" is from *The Toothed and Clever World* (TreeHouse Press, 2006).

pages 17 and 19: "Lapsed Meadow" is from Stanley Plumly's *Summer Celestial* (Ecco/Harper Collins, 1983). "The James Wright Annual Festival" is from Plumly, *Selected Poems: Now That My Father Lies Down Beside Me*, 1970–2000 (Ecco/Harper Collins).

pages 21 and 23: "The Middle Path" and "Last Holy Fragrance," from *Strong Is Your Hold*: Poems by Galway Kinnell. Copyright © 2006 by Galway Kinnell. Reprinted by permission of Houghton Mifflin Company. All rights reserved.

pages 28 and 29: "Sweet Land" and "Isla de Pasqua" are from *No Name Harbor, Poetry of Barbary Chaapel* (PublishAmerica, 2006).

page 30: Christina Lovin is the author of *What We Burned For Warmth*. "Two" appeared in *Liasons II* (Minden Hills Cultural Center, 2007).

page 31: Susan North's "Blue Horses" was first published in *IRONWOOD*, 19, Vol.10, no. 1, Spring `82.

page 33: Gina Tabasso's poems have appeared in numerous literary magazines. She belly dances, rides a thoroughbred, and works as a corporate communications manager in Ohio. "Seeing God" is published here for the first time.

page 35: "The Stallion" is from *The Book of Names: New and Selected Poems*. Copyright © 1993 by Barton Sutter. Reprinted with the permission of the author and BOA Editions, Ltd., www.boaeditions.org.

page 36: "On Learning of a Friend's Illness" from *Collected Poems* by C.K. Williams. Copyright © 2006 by C.K. Williams. Reprinted with permission of Farrar, Straus and Giroux, LLC.

page 39: David Budbill has published numerous collections of poetry, his newest being *While We Still Have Feet*. "Also" appears here for the first time.

page 40: Rick Hilles' *BROTHER SALVAGE* (published by the University of Pittsburgh Press) won the 2005 Agnes Lynch Starrett Prize and was named the 2006 Poetry Book of the Year by *ForeWord* Magazine. He teaches in the MFA Program at Vanderbilt University. "Missoula Eclipse" appears here for the first time.

page 43: Judith Pacht has published in several journals. "Waterville, Maine, Near Great Pond" was one of five winners of the Robinson Jeffers Tor House Prize for Poetry in 2007.

page 45: Bruce Henricksen was one of James Wright's students at the University of Minnesota. "Now, in Minnesota" appears here for the first time.

page 46: Sharon Chmielarz has published four books of poems, her latest being *The Rhubarb King*. She was one of James Wright's students at the University of Minnesota. "The Professor" appears here for the first time.

page 47: Brenton Lee is a nephew of James Wright. His poem, appearing here for the first time, was submitted by Anne Wright.

pages 48 and 50: "With Our Wives in Late October" and "Lost Letter to James Wright, With Thanks for a Map of Fano" are from Gibbons Ruark, *Passing Through Customs: New and Selected Poems* (Louisiana State University Press, 1999).

page 52: Meena Alexander's "House of the Red Canoe" will also appear in *Quick Changing River* (TriQuarterly Books/Northwestern University Press, 2008).

page 53: Diane Kendig has published two chapbooks of her own poetry and a third of translations. "The Trees Near Fiesole" first appeared in *Gambit*, 1985.

pages 54 and 55: Joyce Sutphen won the Barnard New Women's Poetry Prize for *Straight Out of View* (1995) and the Minnesota Book Award for *Naming the Stars* (2004). She teaches at Gustavus Adolphus College in St. Peter, MN. "Going Someplace" appeared originally in *Sidewalks*, whereas "After That" appears here for the first time.

page 56: "Small Miracles" initially appeared in *Connecticut Review*. Wally Swist's poetry can be found in many journals, and in his book, *Veils of the Divine* (Hanover Press, 2003).

page 57: M.J. Iuppa has published three chapbooks and a full-length collection of poems, *Night Traveler* (Foothills Publishing, 2003). "Pond" first appeared in *Rosebud*, no. 28, 2003.

page 58: Ellen Seusy's "The Compost Bin" was published in *I Have My Own Song For It: Poems of Ohio*, ed. Glaser and Williams (University of Akron Press, 2002).

page 60: Thomas R. Smith teaches at the Loft Literary Center in Minneapolis. The latest of his five books is *Waking Before Dawn* (Red Dragonfly Press, 2007). "After Thanksgiving" appears here for the first time.

page 61: Steve Troyanovich is the author of *Dream Dealers and Other Shadows*. "drifting home . . ." appears here for the first time.

page 62: Kate Johnson has authored three collections of poetry, teaches at Sarah Lawrence College in New York, and has a private practice in psychoanalysis.

page 64: Susan Kelly-DeWitt is an editor of Swan Scythe Press. Her first collection of poetry, *The Fortunate Islands*, will be published by Marick Press in 2008. "The Messenger" appears here for the first time.

page 65: Helen Ruggieri is the author of a poetry collection, *Glimmer Girls*, and a collection of prose poems, *The Character for Woman*. "The Kind of Poetry I Want" appears here for the first time.

pages 66 and 68: Michael Dennis Browne's book, *James Wright and Other Essays*, will be published by Carnegie Mellon in 2008. He teaches at the University of Minnesota. "The Voices" and "Shall We Gather" appear here for the first time.

page 69: "Diving For the Drowned" is from *Turning Out the Stones* by Marc Harshman (State Street Press Chapbooks, 1983).

page 71: "First Spring" appeared in Maggie Smith's book, *Lamp of the Body* (Red Hen Press, 2005).

page 73: Tonya Northenor's poems have appeared in numerous journals. "Along the Ohio Valley" is published here for the first time.

page 74: Nancy Paddock's books of poems include *A Dark Light* and *Trust the Wild Heart*. "Snow Goose River" originally appeared in *Women Poets of the Twin Cities* (Vanilla Press).

pages 75 and 76: Robert Bly's "The Canada Goose" was published in *There is No Other Way to Speak* (Minnesota Center for Book Arts, 2005). "A Note on James Wright" first appeared in *IRONWOOD*, vol. 5, no. 2, 1977.

A Brief Bibliography

The standard edition of James Wright's poetry, with an Introduction by Donald Hall, is *Above The River: The Complete Poems* (The Noonday Press, 1990).

An excellent shorter collection is *James Wright: Selected Poems*, edited by Robert Bly and Anne Wright (Farrar, Straus & Giroux, 2005).

A good general introduction is *James Wright: A Profile*, edited by Frank Graziano & Peter Stitt (Logbridge-Rhodes, 1988). This book contains selected poems, critical commentary, interviews, and photographs.

The Poetry of a Grown Man: Constancy and Transition in the Work of James Wright by Kevin Stein (Ohio University Press, 1989) divides Wright's career into three stages of development. Stein's study warrants comparison with Peter Stitt's similar thesis in *James Wright: A Profile*.

Michael Dennis Browne's *James Wright and Other Essays* will be published in 2008 by Carnegie Mellon.

James Wright's papers are at the University of Minnesota in the Anderson Library, Minneapolis.

About Lost Hills Books

LOST HILLS BOOKS launched its career in 2007 in Duluth, Minnesota, its purpose being to publish literary fiction and poetry of the highest quality in small editions of five hundred to two thousand copies. All books will be available from the online sellers and will be placed with the major wholesalers when possible. Submissions will be read by invitation only.

In addition to the poetry collection that you hold in your hand, Lost Hills begins with Bruce Henricksen's novel, *After the Floods*. The story is set in post-Katrina New Orleans and in a fictional Minnesota town that has also suffered a watery disaster. Under the license granted by magical realism, Nature's upheavals have altered the speed of time while giving animals, who observe the human predicament, the power of speech. Occasionally sad and often hilarious, *After the Floods* is ultimately a hopeful tale about survival and recovery.

www.losthillsbooks.com